The Tightrope Wedding

For Kay

Previous publications
Cloves of Garlic (Smith/Doorstop Books, 1989)
Thinking of Happiness (Peterloo Poets, 1991)
In the Fruit Cage (Smith/Doorstop Books, 1997)

Acknowledgements
Thanks are due to the editors of the following publications in which some of these poems first appeared: *Arvon Competition Anthology 1998, Gown Literary Supplement, The Independent, Joe Soap's Canoe, London Magazine, London Review of Books, The North, Other Poetry, Poetry Durham, Poetry London Newsletter, The Rialto, Scratch, Seam, Soundings, The Spectator, Staple, Verse* and *What Poets Eat* (Foolscap, 1994).

The Tightrope Wedding

Michael Laskey

Smith/Doorstop Books

Published 1999 by
Smith/Doorstop Books
The Poetry Business
The Studio
Byram Arcade
Westgate
Huddersfield HD1 1ND

ISBN 1-902382-07-2

A CIP catalogue record for this book is available from the British Library.

Typeset at The Poetry Business
Printed by Peepal Tree Press, Leeds

The cover photograph: 'Couple in Wedding Dress on Tightrope' (photographer unknown) is reproduced with permission from Sygma.
Author's photograph by Roger Bloxham

Distributed by Littlehampton Book Services Ltd, 10-14 Eldon Way, Lineside Estate, Littlehampton BN17 7HE

The Poetry Business gratefully acknowledges the help of
Kirklees Metropolitan Council and Yorkshire & Humberside Arts.

CONTENTS

Home Movies

By the final frame of the film, before
the tinny rattle of a jerked reel
or that dazzle on the bald sitting-room wall,
Dad had leaped up beside the projector

and flicked the switch, so their shaky story
went ratcheting on, only backwards now:
led in by balloons, bouncing cans and clouds
of exhaust, the car came reversing surely

far too fast at the horseshoe of guests
crowding Gran's gravel, and we had to laugh
at the way our would-be father muffed
his entrance, emerging bottom first

to pose for a moment with his right arm
flung round an untarnished version of Mum.
No sound, just a pan of everyone
cracking up, the storm before the calm

delivery by Dad of some old joke.
Hilarious how they all skedaddled
backwards up the steps into the middle
of the reception: a piece of cake

that a waitress snatched; each hopeful wish
promptly returning unopened to sender
as the knife they were forcing up together
lifted off, leaving the icing unblemished;

a quick balancing trick put the tiers in place;
then unedited longueurs – little movement,
too many self-conscious close-ups of distant
relations and friends they'd lost without trace

and whom we'd never known – nothing comical
except for a slim-line uncle Jim
brightening as glass after glass of his wine
vanished, sucked up by the mouth of the bottle.

It was round about then, while we were all
full of it, paralytic at him
sobering up, that Mum left the room
with a kind of abruptness that niggled

(or would have, if we'd adjusted our focus,
not chosen not to notice) and so she missed
what followed: their ceremonial kiss
outside the church; Dad reaching across

to conceal her face with the antique veil;
and once the blinking guests had withdrawn
into the dark doorway arm in arm
he steered her backwards, helped by two small

bridesmaids tugging her train in towards
the vestry, the moment when he'd unscrew
his pen and one by one they'd undo
their signatures, going over the words

from right to left so they disappeared,
and suddenly the twinkle in Dad's eye
was a hard gleam in the flickering light
and the rare warmth of the atmosphere

too close: not one of us raised the ghost
of a laugh as Dad softly eased the ring
off the finger so gladly held out to him,
or dared interrupt to point out the past

was spilling out, already ankle-deep
on the floor and spreading. He stood so still
we didn't exist. There was nothing real
but that slither of negatives at his feet.

Auntie

(1902-1998)

Among the stuff in her room
this album turned up. Slid under
the cellophane on page one
her message: *This book is for Kay*
and here we are, dated, arranged,
on the beach, in front of the Cabin,
the boys wearing clothes I'd forgotten
yet my fingers can still feel the weave
and weight of, tops I could ease
gently over their ears in my sleep.
Here's Jack's green Clothkits tracksuit,
Tim's slinky red shorts, Ben's tough cords.
Our first ten years in Suffolk
when Auntie still drove and came up
with old nursing friends every summer.
Their names are on the tip of my tongue:
Gam. Barbara. Dorothy Menassah
piggybacking Tim over the pebbles.
And Auntie not appearing of course
except on the first and last pages
where she's put herself out of the wind
in the porch with a cup and saucer,
the Cabin's everlasting plain blue.
She'd a soft spot for backs. Here's one
of us pushing our bikes down the slatted
wooden walkway, heading off home.
But whenever she calls we look up
smiling warmly, perfectly natural.

The Last Swim

September, October ... one thing
you don't know at the time is when
you've had your last swim: the weather
may hold, may keep nudging you in.

Only afterwards, sometimes days on,
it dawns on you that you've done:
just the thought of undressing outdoors,
exposing bare skin, makes you wince.

And that's best, to have gone on swimming
easily to the end: your crawl
full of itself, and the future
no further than your folded towel.

First Test

At the Oval this afternoon England
are in real trouble: 19-4
as Laskey joins May at the wicket
and takes guard. The youngest player
ever selected for England, facing
his first ball from Lindwall. An absolute
stillness. Lindwall bowls, a full length,
Laskey's forward and, pushing it wide
of the drain at mid-off, finds the gap
by the coal-shed out into the passage.
Perfectly timed. Four runs. Fetching the ball
from beside the back door, he can't help
hearing the wireless, the Mau Mau
have murdered another white settler
and his wife overnight on their farm
near Murang'a just north of Nairobi.

Simpson and Newell

Not blessed by the flu or a freak
frost or storm, we climbed down
from the coach there, queasy, disturbed
by how solid they looked, how puny
our voices came out in the open.

We fell in behind and trailed them,
swinging the lightly clenched fists
of our kitbags through chinese whispers:
the score they'd run up at Culford
where we'd just clung on for a draw.

Corridors of cocksure staring
boys for a moment diverted
by our appearance; a scummy
courtyard muscled with drainpipes;
in the changing room half the pegs

decapitated. Left to ourselves
we unzipped a little flamboyant
foul language and let it drop
into shallow pooled laughter; we bolted
the bog doors and sat briefly, slumped.

Trying not to think about Simpson
or Newell, we forced our heads
through our hooped shirts, knotted our shorts
and the laces we'd wound and braced
round our ankles and under our insteps.

But knew all the time they were loping
relentlessly towards us, spin-
passing, their hands as appallingly
sure as the referee's watch-hands,
as those chirpy blasts on his whistle.

We lost I'm sure. I can remember
diving hopelessly after Simpson
as he lengthened his stride and went past,
such casual power in his thighs.
Just boys we were, fifteen, sixteen.

And afterwards, quiet on the coach
returning to school through the settled
ache of that bruise-darkened landscape,
we breathed on the window and printed
our names in the mist back to front.

Then

Then there were the chickens, a couple
of dozen mum kept for their colours,
the kerfuffle they added to the garden,
as much as for the eggs that we'd take
turns to collect, lifting the lid
on the nesting box, sometimes surprising
a bird sitting tight whose black eye
and beak we soon learned to defy.
They were ours, all the eggs we found
and carried like the eucharist back
indoors in the cracked china bowl.
When we banged on the grain tin they'd come
running, not Spot, but the rest,
scampering, flapping from the far
ends of the garden. They'd feed
from our cupped hands. They clucked
in our mother tongue. Natural to us –
dried droppings and squit underfoot,
the ammoniac stink of the hen-house
where we shut them up safely each dusk,
all except Spot with her neck
pecked bare and the flesh round her blind
right eye always raw who roosted
in the lean-to alongside the garage
among rusty buckets, smashed cloches.

Nude

Why is he wearing no clothes?
Not for love you can tell by his limp
penis, his scrotum drawn in
tight, I suppose from the cold.
Nor for money: imagine paying
for the pleasure of viewing the slack
of that lopsided stomach, the odd
threadbare look of those legs.

A body that's seen better days,
flesh we'd both rather see dressed.
For though he keeps his mouth closed,
endures perhaps by fending off words,
his posture is speaking – head
ducked, shoulders hunched, arms crossed,
an elbow clasped in a hand –
foolishly, meekly, bleakly

waiting for an explanation
of why his clothes have been taken.
For plainly he'd never have chosen
to appear like this among strangers,
exposing the imprint of pants
round his waist and these white knees,
so soft and bald from their years
of rubbing along inside trousers.

And he won't go away: he's lost
property, nameless, his wrist
barely remembering the light
pressure of his fancied watch.
But why stand here at the bottom
of my stairs, souring my air?
Why can't he put on these clothes
of mine? Can I be to blame?

What the Cut Said

Don't ask me how serious I am,
I'm numb still, you numbskull. Go on –
tug the glove off and see what you've done.

* *

Accident? When you let the hedge
grow so high and couldn't be bothered
to secure the foot of the ladder?

* *

I'm a thoughtless remark you've made
that you can't take back. At the cold
tap, your precious sensibility's stinging.

* *

You call this pain? Just as well
there's codeine upstairs and no cause
you can rat on to save your skin.

* *

Not the wild hedge mastered. Instead
me to nurse and carry around
all day, your whimpering child.

* *

Though steristrips gag me and gauze
binds me up firmly, I'm still
protesting, I'll trouble your sleep.

* *

So quick to forgive yourself
and expecting sympathy too –
I'd be scared if I were you.

* *

It took me to teach you how much
you depend on this fingertip. Don't
forget it or I'll make you yelp.

* *

I'm your own fault, proof you're inept
you laugh off. Now the plaster's gone
you turn a blind eye to my grin.

Heads: Studies for a Self-Portrait

A purse with small change and a bobble of fluff
A planet I'm planning one day to land on
A 15-watt light bulb left burning all night
A paddock with horseshit, mushrooms and thistles
A pond with sludge taking ages to settle
A brown screwtop bottle tightly done up
      A hall of mirrors

A bait-digger's bucket, glistening with lug
A porous boulder embedded with fossils
A camera that may or may not have a film in
A pot of strong coffee not letting me sleep
A spin dryer trying out novel positions
A smooth dome enclosing nuclear fission
      A cave to crouch in

A saucer with curtain hooks, buttons, a screw
A moored boat swung back and forth on the tide
A mid-terraced house going back miles
A balloon gone soft that puckers when touched
A freezer packed with cuts of raw meat
A coal scuttle, down to a shovel of slack
      A crucible fuming

A rocket en route to the stratosphere
A wire trap scrabbled by a frantic rat
A cot a forgotten child jiggles and kicks
A saucepan rattled by mussels opening up
A thermos flask keeping a grudge good and hot
A demijohn intermittently plopping
      A medicine cupboard

An empty oil-drum pitted with rust
A gutter in the grip of lascivious sparrows
A pepper mill speckling every dish
A skip I keep checking, just in case
A wasps' nest, a natural at self-defence
A whirlpool swallowing all-comers
      A sitting duck

Honouring the Memory

It's mine I want to honour,
the natural way it copes
with hurt, remorse or grief
and swallows scalding horror.

Here, whistling to myself
and strolling in the spring
sunshine, hands in pockets,
I'm obviously blessed

with a good one, given
what took place last month.
I knew that I'd forget it
if I didn't write it down.

The Day After

I made a leek and potato soup
the day after, prompted by the look
of the peeled potato going soft
in a glass of water by the sink.
Beyond the back door, drizzle
and the raw morning air argued for soup,
added their weight to the nod of the knife
slicing the leeks, wrapped up in themselves,
into logs, into rings – whites, yellows and greens –
that I agitated till they came clean
in a bowl of cold water and set
simmering with the potato in stock
I'd thickened with flour, sprinkled with dried
herbs – rosemary, thyme – and startled
with a splash of leftover wine.
We had it for lunch, liquidised
with the top of the milk and heated through
and though I dare say you didn't notice
the taste, you ate it. It's sometimes too soon
to speak about things, but you've got to eat.

The Burn

Putting the honey to warm on the boiler
to soften it for his slice of toast
and feeling the blessed heat on his face
this cold morning he must have reached out
his hand, instinctively drawn to the vibrant
silver flue.
           I'd sooner not think
of his fingers like solder, his speechless pain
that brought us running from separate rooms
to soothe him with hydrocortisone cream
and a timely bandage wrapped round and round.
No hockey. No rock guitar class. No flute
for a week at least.
           But though it still hurts –
he's taken painkillers with him to school –
it's already healing, won't scar, won't be
remembered at all by the end of the war.

A Family Joke

Just her superstition – never
to watch a guest pass out of sight.
There we'd be all waving together
till the last moment when she'd turn

and dash indoors. Not that it dawned on us
for years – she was just our mother –
but rumbling her we were unanimous:
nonsense like that had to stop.

So we'd encourage her, slip our arms
around her shoulders and then hold her
more firmly the more she squirmed;
and she'd be laughing, but wouldn't look.

And still won't. We watch her duck
inside the porch as we drive away,
don't scoff so much at the bad luck
she wouldn't risk bringing down on us.

Driving Home

You're on your own driving home,
the miles light music that you spool
from wheel to wheel. Each dip and bend
hums with the tune. It's late at night
and, though you're tired, it's not far now:
the glow shows up across the fields.

A thud, a simultaneous crunch,
and, as you stamp on brakes and wrench
hard at the wheel, a scrape, a thump.
The reeling darkness stalls and drops
a lump of terror in your lap.
The car has shuddered to a stop

facing backwards and across,
so what you see is this: lit up
beside the verge, a buckled bike
and in the ditch beyond, a heap
of tangled clothes. Nothing moves.
A country road. No other lights

in sight but yours. And what you think
at once is this: no witnesses.
You're stunned, appalled. What's to be done?
You can't park where you are. Reverse.
Whatever damage to the wing
it's not caved in. The car still steers.

You know it's dangerous to move
some injuries. You hesitate.
You've never been much good with blood.
Still no-one comes. It might make sense
to drive fast to the nearest house
and use their phone. You must fetch help.

The first place – now you think of it
as you slow down – 's a second home:
it looks shut up, hedge overgrown.
The next's for sale. The third's a farm
down a rough track, two fields back,
a cert for early nights, and dogs.

You check your mirror. Up ahead
no looming lights. No traffic still.
The big house on the corner's black
against the sky. A waste of time.
To pull those distant sleepers back
a bell would have to shrill and shrill.

You had no warning, never saw him.
It makes you wonder. You were driving
well, not wildly; you'd remember
any twitch of fright or tightness
on that bend. You would have braked.
What's likely is he had no lights.

One gleaming window seen too late
– already past and going too fast –
makes you dither, lift your foot,
but then the thought that any light
left shining out along this route
might burn for nothing but that bike

settles it. Why knock and call
through bolted doors, unlock alarm
in narrow halls, explain, explain,
when little more than three miles on,
the other side of this small town,
you'll be beside your phone, at home?

The streets are hollow, brightly lit.
A stray dog cocks a leg and sniffs
along a fence. A couple kiss
persistently. A street-lamp blinks.
A van pulls out ahead, turns right
and, unremarked, you roll straight on.

You kill the engine, douse the lights
and sit a moment in the dark
breathing out. Hot metal ticks.
What's done is done. You know a man
who'll fix the car. Softly you close
the up-and-over garage door.

Bike

You, who have borne three sons
of mine, still bear my weight
routinely, transporting me.

An odd pair: your classic spare
lines – elbows, bony frame –
and me, bearlike, cumbersome,

nosing tangled coils of air
you cut through with your pure
purposeful geometry.

With you it's feet off the ground,
a feat passing unremarked
though in full public view.

Keeping each other's balance.
Our talk slow recurrent clicks,
companionable creaks.

Through you I've come to know
winds inside out and raw
weather ignored before;

and nuances of slopes,
the moving earth, green tracks
for blackberries and sloes

for gin, for jam: the tug
and tang of fruit pulling me
clear of the wheel of myself.

Sloes

Our bikes on the verge behind us
bowled over by bush after bush
so lavish with sloes we can't stop
picking them, the powder blue bloom
dissolving wherever we touch
and the glossy black showing through.
They've come a long way from the starry
white flowers they were on bare wood
in the early spring. We roll handfuls
into the plastic bag
I've emptied of spanners and bits
and pieces of puncture repair kits
and turned inside out. Later on
we'll prick them one by one
and steep them in sugar and gin
for months, giving the bottles
a brisk shake every so often.
But for now it's us they're filling,
even to our fingertips stubbed
by pressing phone calls and faxes
they're giving back feeling. I see
your pupils darkening with love.

Marmalade

January again, and again
the Sevilles won't wait. If I'm not
quick, they'll be going off.

So I fetch my sharpest
knife, my favourite
blue and white plate

and halve them, quarter them, cut
slices so thin every pip's
conspicuous, can be picked out

and kept for its pectin; nothing's
wasted, the rest of it pressed
into the mincer, screwed through.

My hands sting from the juice:
pinpricks that open their mouths
and rejoice that they've been pointed out.

Jack wants to help, and this time
he can turn the handle with ease:
he's minced up a whole twelve months.

The fruit steeps overnight
in the pan. We're going to be pounds
better off when we wake.

I set it simmering to soften
the peel and now every room's
filled with its tart aroma.

The clutter of empty jars
shunted to the back of the cupboard
gleam, coming into their own.

With the sugar dissolved there's nothing
else but this full rolling boil
pelting the windows with steam.

On the bottom lip of the spoon
at last a drop hesitates, sets.
Is it time to pot, or too soon?

Until it's quite cold I won't know:
while the cellophane tops tighten,
I tilt between hope and despair.

The Present

Poking about in the garage
for tacks to patch up the flapping
felt on the roof I can't not
notice the bat-box. Last summer
he made it. That's six whole months
it's lain on the shelf, all my passing
thoughts swerving unerringly off.
Yet such a cinch to put up:
the holes ready drilled; the required
nails still taped on, like a spray
of slender grey flowers for a wedding;
and certainly somewhere indoors
the Nature Conservancy Council
pamphlet he lent me on bats,
advice on choosing a site.
So thoroughly green – he's used nothing
but off-cuts of untreated wood –
and so diligent, it makes me sick
of myself, my sloth, this life-
size mock-up of my head with its knots,
its slit, tight lid and misplaced
dark void that might have provided
for pipistrelles, say, or noctules.

The Washing

My head's revolving the same
familiar soiled clothes. Why not
drop the sneck on the lot and stride off
purposefully out of earshot?

* *

But someone must unruck those socks,
check pockets and give a brisk rub
at grease spots, at collars and cuffs.
I moan sometimes making love.

* *

There are thoughts that pick you up
and exhilarate you like surf;
and there's sorting the clothes and deciding
which pile to wash first.

* *

Dull today – yet I know exactly
how long the tap takes to run hot
and find myself coming on cue
as the final spin cuts out.

* *

Your silence is striking, you're waiting
for me to loosen your tongue,
to draw out the tangled coils
of your morning flung round the drum.

* *

The ways one can vary the line –
hanging odd socks in between
upside down shirts, grouping runs
of legs, stripes, rectangles, greens.

* *

They're yours, these damp pants, this purple
tee-shirt I grip by the seams
and tug so often I seldom
remember I know where they've been.

* *

Out of sight, but not quite out of mind –
if the window darkens with spatters
of rain, I drop everything, dash
out. Nothing else matters.

* *

But even now filling my arms
with this good drying day, as it folds
in on itself, I'm nonplussed
at the blank spaces left by our clothes.

Small World

At seven he's known no other home:
playground, playgroup, primary school,
the shops, and Christopher and Joe
minutes away on the handed down
red and blue Raleigh Rodeo
that he rattles along beside me on
these days. The tyres seldom need
pumping; the rust's just superficial.

All going well, but once in a while
he remembers Zack, a boy in his class
last year who left, who moved house.
We try to picture that natty jacket.
His dad apparently owned four phones,
could always be contacted. Not like Zack.

Piano Practice

It's something I like you to find
me doing when you come home;
only sometimes it so absorbs me
that glancing up I can't think
straight off who you are or how come
you're standing there in that doorway.

But normally, knowing the joy
of doing it and the certain
blight of putting it off,
I put it off. There are always
other things, these windows
for instance that still need cleaning.

Now it's the children's turn
to do what they can. Let their fingers
release the chords shut inside
so long they're quite stiff and lift off
only with difficulty. Children,
come on, do come on, we're expecting
great things.

You'd swear you were watching a boy
bouncing a ball on a wall,
but I know better: it's Ben
not practising.

Not a lie, just an embellishment,
a slight improvement on the truth:
it's not giving up the piano,
more wanting to take up the flute.

The Rabbits

Weakness to have kept them I think.
What are they but one short-lived
stage the boys went through
ages ago and abandoned?

Yet keep them I do. Still soothed
by stroking them; still attached
to their dumb dependence perhaps.
Not a hint of reproach in my voice

as I call up the stairs or cut
in over the tele to tell them
I'm outside seeing to the rabbits
and they'll have to answer the phone.

The Light

At mid-morning seeing the light
in his bedroom still on, the blinds down,
I swear out loud, earmark him
for a piece of my mind. Three hours
it's been on. Three hours since he left
for school and in all that time

I haven't thought of him once.
A tug and the blind rolls up
on itself, admits the dazzle
of days when I ached with love
that I'd point his way as he began
number work, playtime, packed lunch.

Double-take

Next to mine on the basin, his stick
of Palmolive. Not worn on the skew
like mine, not hollowed out by hard pushed
latherings, but tenderly brushed
to a tip, so I see it at once:
with the silver paper peeled back
it's a penis, a perfect green prick.

I must watch myself, be on my guard
against pretexts, smooth as new blades,
for cutting the boy down to size.

The Knife

You brought it with you to the marriage
I think, already in your kitchen drawer
in Savernake Road when we first
pooled our possessions. A perfectly
ordinary kitchen knife: the two
rivets through the dark stained wood
of the handle still holding the blade
firmly after twenty years. Signs
of wear though, as you'd expect: the tip
broken off – used as a lever once
too often – a nick in the edge
and the brown handle mottled, streaked
unevenly where the wood dye's leached.
I like it sharp: gritting my teeth
I grind it between steel wheels
now and again, scare my thumb.
It fits my fist, loves stringing beans,
slicing onions, tomatoes, courgettes.
Who'd have thought it would come to matter
so much to me, this small knife
you say now you're not sure was yours?

Ratatouille

was a revelation, like the simmering
colours of your room that first time:
the purple wall hung with fine
cane blinds; the Indian bedspread;
the cracked basin airing your damp
green flannel; the planks and the bricks
for Lawrence, Sartre, Dostoyevsky,
and others I could see would be
quite beyond me – Gray's Anatomy,
Surgery by Bailey and Love.
I'd never eaten them before
that evening, aubergines. Or courgettes.
Did I even know what they were called?
You unfolded a table and lit
a candle. We sat with our knees
almost touching. Every so often
we paused, forks poised, held our peace
as a train clattered past, shook the glass.
Later on you must have taught me
how to make it, though I still don't get
the chemistry, why salt on the slices
draws out the bitter juices
or why the colours, tastes and textures
blend better, stir me more year by year.

The Visitation

It was Kay sleeping that woke me.
For once she was breathing so deeply,
so slowly, I had to break surface.

From the landing I heard a movement
downstairs, in the sitting-room surely,
like a cartilage clicking, the rocking-

chair maybe, but nothing alarming
or furtive, so I stood in the open
doorway and switched on the light.

'I took out the bulb' said a voice
that had to be Mick's. 'There's a moth
I've been taking some photos of here

and I don't want it burnt. Come and see.'
Through the darkness he reached an arm
round my shoulder and pointed the beam

of his torch on the curtain in the bay
where a small moth clung, its green wings
intricately speckled and veined

white and black. There was no need to speak
about Lesley or why he'd left them.
Or why I'd written just once.

'It's a Merveille du Jour' he told me.
'Not at all rare.'

Separations

The old story: the years we've spent
learning, earning one another,
the times our eyes met intimately over
the heads of the children no longer
      count.

    **

Mum was there to collect me at close
of play. On my seat someone's stray
hairgrip I was quick to bury
in a pocket, so we wouldn't worry
      whose.

    **

His secretary, colleague, chance
acquaintance. Years younger than he is.
A zest he can't quite disguise,
a spring in his step I didn't despise
      once.

    **

Though he showed me the place he'd park,
when they let me out early the car
had disappeared. God knows where
Dad spent that hour. I didn't dare
      ask.

    **

I watch him leaving, driving off.
He won't look back. I'm the ghost
that's driven him away, his past
haunted by our happiness, his first
      wife.

    **

When he went, did he think of this?
The way I'd groan under the weight
of her grief, her grievances, the slight
pressure of each brave goodnight
      kiss.

    **

If not us, what might hold him? Shame?
The seed of a doubt about self-
fulfilment? Old friend, can this help –
me doing my best with these half-
        rhymes?

The Apple Trees

So much I don't know. It's plain
the trees are diseased, but whether
it's leaf curl, droop, blotches or mites
I can't tell from the book.
Is it potash they need, or lime
forked lightly in last autumn?
Should I cut out and burn or wait
for a still evening and spray them
with derris? Or pyrethrum perhaps?
So much I don't know that the trees
better not be depending on me.

The Bonfire

More than the sum of its parts –
grass cuttings, elder, laurel –
the bonfire keeps burning.

All week we feed it, spring-cleaning
flowerbeds and paths, and pruning
the worst of the shrubs with a saw.

Barrowloads we've upended
on top – forkfuls of weeds and clods
of earth, impossibly matted –

and it works its way through the lot,
with us hardly intervening
at all, just heaping the stuff

back on top from time to time.
This morning, after that rain
in the night, we look dully out

weighed down by the clouds, but a twist
of irrepressible smoke
lifts me like one of your jokes.

Self-heal

Self-heal she found and ground ivy,
common sorrel, common stork's bill and fresh
nettles, nothing extraordinary,
except now she was hooked. New tendrils
extended her, drew her out often,
held her steady with biro and pad
logging the changes in her chosen
patch of waste ground. The foundation
course in science she wouldn't discuss
with anyone then, wouldn't even
mention to Mike just in case
it didn't take. It was her secret
attachment. He hadn't a clue
what it meant to her learning the names
of the grasses, telling tall fescue
from timothy and tufted hair.
Couldn't start to guess how upset
she'd be by the cuttings from the hedge
he raked up while he thought of it
that Saturday morning and lit.

Sailing Lessons

It was learning the term that helped:
a building or trees on the bank
cast what they called a wind-shadow
over the water, extending
ten times the obstruction's height.

It could stop the wind dead, set the boat
rocking wildly, might even capsize you.
So at last it made sense, he tensed
himself for the lull ahead,
the weekend at home with his Dad.

Passenger

I'm back in the back sometimes now
that Ben drives. I peer out between
the headrests, uneasy at first
at how fast it all feels. Eighteen

already, and coming up so close
to the car in front we'll be flung
about when he swings out to pass it.
I brace myself, hold my tongue.

He's confident though, knows the road
and doesn't take risks. A few miles
and my phantom grip on the wheel
relaxes, I tick over, idle.

He's changing gear smoothly. I slot
my hands in my pockets and settle
to these novel peripheral views:
culverts, cloudscapes, a kestrel.

In front they're talking, their voices
take turns, change pitch, but the words
are blurred by the engine's vibrations;
to join in I'd have to lean forwards.

But I'm warm here and drifting off,
lulled by the whop of the cars
passing, a boy being driven
home surely by my father.

Putting Things Right

So simple it could be, like choosing
to stop swimming lengths and to duck
under the taut orange rope
on its red, white and blue plastic floats
into free swimming, where the boys
sleek as seals are diving to retrieve
locker keys, waving them aloft,
and Dad in the shallow end's backing
away from me, nodding and calling
'Keep kicking! Keep kicking! Well done.'
But however wildly I splash
there's no disguising the fact
I can swim already and one thing's
certain – he won't like that.

Pudding

For years she tried to get it right,
off and on. No cinnamon,
she learnt, and less vanilla essence.
A pinch of nutmeg, half an ounce
more sugar than it said, not brown –
as she'd used once – but caster.

It was his favourite, so she made it
often and achieved such moistness
in the middle and a skin
so delicate and thickly freckled
he was baffled, just couldn't say
the way his mum's had differed.

At last she'd asked her – it was after
Olga died, when all that sadness
softened them – and she admitted
that what she did was add a little
tin of Ambrosia Creamed Rice.
It's been fresh fruit ever since.

Knowing One's Place

On the tarmac outside the back door
an ordinary kitchen chair:
a pleasure to come on it there,
feet on the ground and surrounded
by all this open air.
I listen to it quietly, stay still,
willing you not to emerge
with your window-cleaning gear
or a plank, an explanatory saw.

If not in the presence of God,
at least aware of our chairs:
whatever happens, however
unsettled our affairs, their laps
cradle our buttocks and backs,
they take the unspeakable weight
off our feet. Oh, what have we done
to deserve to be understood
by chairs, by so many good chairs?

Home unexpectedly early,
I surprised my motley lot
arranged round the kitchen table
conferring – the pair of windsors,
the ladderback, the slim
cane-seat Mum passed on.
They clammed up at once, but the silence
hummed with their puzzled agreement
that they'd none of them meant to be chairs.

What's hardest for a chair to bear?
Despite all my warnings, not a boy
tilting one backwards: its splat
creaking's neither here nor there
for a normal chair; in fact better
to be under a little external

pressure than bored by the worm
or, worse still, lost in the hall
where no-one will ever sit down.

But standing here dumbly,
while birds fling their confetti of song
into the room, while sunlight –
striking through the heart of the beech –
flickers on the faded gold
leaf-patterned upholstered seat
of the Hepplewhite, you too might almost
sense it flinch, diminished: never
to be anything, except a chair.

Small Town Life

Mispronounced it probably that first time
I drove through, and had no idea,
not an inkling we'd end up living here.
A hole – mercifully small was the thought
that crossed my mind as it vanished behind.

Cut off for those two days, a perfect
island. The snow had drifted, closed
the schools, disconnected the milk, the post.
We pulled our sledge down the middle of the road,
our heads in the clouds we were breathing out.

Why does it please me so much seeing
these two together and knowing at once
they must be related? It's a resemblance
I never noticed in years of passing them
one at a time: such a nice rhyme.

I know him too, in the bus shelter crew,
a shy boy who'd settle on my knee
in the reading corner, who easily
outstares me now – abashed by his cool
plume of smoke, his bold blank look.

On evenings like this, with November winds
jostling cumulonimbus, the town's
nothing: a ruck of roofs, no-one around,
in the yellow chip shop the television
on its high shelf entertaining itself.

Small enough to walk all the way
round the edge between coffee and lunch.
And never unchanged. Oaks have unclenched.
Tractors make tracks and a lapwing lifts
my head from this heap of sugar-beet.

So now it's you moving. The house,
which I'd thought of simply as yours,
is announcing itself: the For Sale board
clear and inviting. You'll be emptying
shelves soon, striding through hollow rooms.

I consider it too, late at night,
as I do the milk and look east
at the glow the fierce lights broadcast
now over Sizewell: a changed horizon
that proves the town's already moved.

Sometimes at weekends a small lull
comes over the garden and stops
me digging. In the silence far off
I can hear them on the old works field,
yelling hoarsely for a pass, oddly close.

Believing in Heaven

Like coming home from a summer
holiday, that's how I sometimes
saw it: that moment of silence
when the engine dies and the car
settles on the gravel, so benign
that even the outburst of children
quarrelling over the door-key
turns easily into a smile.
A safe arrival, the miles
loosening their grip on my hands.
Unbelting myself, I invent
movement, discovering how stiff
I'd grown, how fast I'd been welded
to the pedals and the bucket seat.
Those scintillating leaves and the whish
of a small bird flitting overhead
make clear what it can be to hear.
And as I remembered, but more so –
more solid, more detailed – the house
welcomes me in with a line
of coat-hooks and space for the cases.
Letters to sort. The kettle
stirring. The boiler igniting,
aroused by the thought of all that
washing. And the grass so lush
it needs a new word, must be trodden
tenderly on, like first snow.
What settled prospects, what harvests
ahead of us in the veg patch.

That's how I used to imagine
it might be, assuming we'd all
feel much the same about home.

Nineteen Minutes

Nineteen minutes, that's all it took him
from the hospital car park home.
It was six when he left her as usual,
a time when the traffic in town's
always thick, but this evening the lights
stayed green till he reached them or changed
from red when he went to slow down.
Not that he drove fast – you don't
at his age and with his iffy heart.
But he wasn't stopped once, not even
at the roundabout by Pearl Assurance
where you join the main road – a lorry
turning right blocked the flow, let him out.
Eleven miles, and yet not the slightest
congestion. Straight through the city
centre, an A road, a B road,
a single track lane. It must mean
something, he thought, as he noted
the time on the dash, the foolish
phut-phut of hope starting up.

Common House

At last after tea it was murder.
With two sets of stairs and a good
number of rooms each side
of the central hallway and landing,
their house was ideal. You could lurk
at the foot of the backstairs, behind
the scullery door, keyed up
for someone to come, that exquisite
panicky gasp when they sensed
breathing, a bulk in the blackness.
Or pad from room to room hunting
a chance or a chosen victim:
Ann, your hectic young cousin,
keen to be cornered and strangled,
or Ste, too intent on spreading
alarm himself to be wary.
Or you'd doom them all to the dark
indefinitely, doing nothing
but grin, trap shut, as the tension
tightened, a temper perhaps snapped.
At other times you'd keep close –
for safety, you'd hiss, trying not
to snort as they backed smartly off –
to Mum and Aunt Nin, the twin
ends of their cigarettes lending
a breathtaking glow to their throats.
Aiming at the perfect crime,
a clean getaway before the corpse's
scream stopped you short and brought you
blinking to the lounge, composed
for the straight-eyed detective.

I remembered all this tonight,
us, them and Uncle Len
every Boxing Day creeping about,
how we'd lie, trying not to laugh.
I was on my way home, coming back
from my latest visit. She looked well,
I'd said, meeting her eye
calmly, ignoring how red
the therapy's making her neck.

54

The Jig

Left for the station in plenty
of time. Carried his case for him
through to the platform, insisted on
doing it, and duly swung it
aboard. Then shrugged off his awkward
thanks, squeezed his shoulder and soberly
waved as the train slid forward,
picking up speed, pulling his long
suffering elsewhere. And so I emerged
onto the car park, into the clear
morning air and found my feet
shamelessly dancing a wild little jig.

Sports Day

Lastly it's the Senior Boys
4 x 110
yard relay, so even though
it's been an interminably
eventful afternoon,
and though I don't know who's who
or which house I'm meant to be
supporting, I'm on my feet,
tense for the gun, and can see
they're men, all four of them, running
so hard round the bend the lanes
can barely contain them, so fast
it makes me gasp. This track's
the whole round world. Four more
reach back already
for the batons and hare away
to the next small strung-out group.
No way of telling who's out
in front while they're still staggered,
but leaving the final muddled
change behind and leading
into the straight, incredibly
it's Uncle Len – so clear
that no-one can touch him now –
with every stride growing taller,
broader, bursting with life.

Hunting the Thimble

We wait in the hall to be called.
Uncle Len gets there first, he jams up
the entrance, poking his head
round the door, asking 'are you quite sure
you're ready now?', eyes all the time
travelling around the room,
while we're shoving him from behind,
protesting, helpless with laughter.
Once we burst in, we begin
glancing high and low, guessing
what it signifies, where whoever's
hidden it has chosen to sit,
watching out for a clue from their eye
movements, and trying to keep track
of the others too, not to miss
any giveaway stillness at the moment
of discovery. But if no-one finds it
at once, we start to settle,
forgetting ourselves as we check
picture-rails, bookshelves, the vaseful
of tulips, the ashen grey tip
of the poker. The sitting-room's
stiff with all of us standing,
our peering heads at odd angles.
But won over by our patient
scrutiny, it slips us a few
suggestions for when it's our go:
that catch on the window, the sockets
round the back of the TV. Not
this time though. Tim's already
sat down with his triple-top smile:
we were looking straight at it before,
but we're cold now, getting colder.

Picking Raspberries with My Mother

So little time left to talk
and arrange things that I must ask her
now when we've hardly begun
picking the raspberries whether
she's thought about what to do
afterwards. She's holding out
the family size Nescafé jar
we're sharing and though I take care
I spill one or two as I funnel
the first handful in, cast down
by my clumsiness. She'll just come home,
she says, turning her attention
back to the canes, not keen
to discuss it. This'll be the last
picking – some are shrivelled already
and the rest, mostly small and pippy,
cling on so the trick is not
to squash them pulling them off.
I gauge the resistance, the give
of each berry between my fingers
and thumb, and press on. It's a big
operation, I say, bending down
and peering among leaves and the pricklish
stems I push back. Let's not think
about it, she shudders. But picturing
the tubes she'll sprout, the drip feed,
I clear my throat. She won't be up
to cooking and shopping. She'll need
to go somewhere for convalescence,
a week or two till she can cope.
But she won't be pressed, won't look
beyond the sagging cage, her worry
one jar's not enough for the boys.
We've been working different rows
side by side so I know she's picking
some I wouldn't touch, like that one –
dulled purple, bobbles so soft

they're mush on her fingers she's forced
to flick into the pot. Extra
sweet, she smiles. I bite my tongue.

Home in Suffolk next morning a note
from Tim, who came in too late
for supper with the rest of us:
Delicious raspberries x x x

The Secret

I was fifty before I knew it,
clearing up stuff after shutting
the oven door on a supper
Tim couldn't wait for. In such
a rush that he'd had to cook
himself an omelette. The secret,
according to him, is to chop
up the onion, bacon and garlic
as small as you can. As he lifted
it out with the fish slice, I found
myself hovering by him, my hand
itching to pick up the pan
and plunge it ebullient in the still
washing-up water. Startled
never to have given this moment
its due before, wondering at Tim
thrusting it flamboyantly in.

Doing My Mother's Ironing

My turn now. I spread the board's
awkward legs on the vinyl floor
of her kitchen – sensible dark
blue squares picked out in grey lines
I've never focused before
in so many years. Like how
exactly you iron, which end
of the shirt you start, perplexed
by tucks, cuffs, sleeves' double ply.
Yet constant, this creak of the pressed
board, the flecked flex scuffing,
the tick of the iron heating up
or cooling, and always the same
smell of hot cotton given off
by this candy-striped blouse
of hers now. Fleshing out
those shadowy movements, I nose
round the buttons, slip a shoulder over
the pointed end and push on,
easing out creases, driving
back and forth to the ward, her worn
smile. She could do with a new
cover – her silver one's tarnished –
and the mat's shedding flakes of what must
be asbestos. But finished for now
I feel for the catch, need to duck
under to see how it works,
how to stand it upright, this stiff
dancing partner I fold
an arm round and walk to the cupboard
under the stairs where it lives.

The Clothes-peg

How it had happened they neither of them knew
but it only got worse. He hated the blank
blue ice of his stare and she couldn't bear
her thin voice telling him to turn
down the TV please, to stop diddling
with that clothes-peg, which without thinking he
clipped to the hem of her cardigan hanging
over the newel post as he mooched past.
It was Margaret at work who pointed it out
and all day it kept on taking her hand
by surprise, a bump in her cardigan pocket.
So naturally closing his old Noah's Ark
curtains that evening she pegged them together.
A few mornings later it waylaid her
inside her shoe. She snapped it on the end
of his toothbrush handle, so it wouldn't pull through
the holder, and found it next clipping the ear
of Humph, her venerable bear. For him she left it
dangling in the dark from the plastic light pull
in the bathroom, where he lit on the pot
of Paracetamol and dibbled it in.
It felt like a biro caught in his train pass
as he brought it out to show the guard,
and tugging a Kleenex out of the box
she spluttered at the clatter, but said nothing,
just hung it from the lining inside his tie
ready for the morning. And now the drizzle starts
as she's driving to work, she laughs out loud –
lifted by it skimming back and forth
riding on the stalk of the wiper blade.

Clock Work

Given their odd spasmodic
talk, their unruly movements –
her tugging at the curtain or him
inserting himself in a shirt –
I prefer the hours spent on my own,
at one with the sunshine swinging
slowly round the room, the minute
gradations from daylight to darkness.

But at night the twelve evenly spaced
luminous dots of my perfectly
circular face and my slim
painted hands glow towards them.
It's touching to watch them – switched off,
breathing slowly, rarely stirring,
their lumpy unfinished faces
softened, an ungainly hand
limp on the stripey duvet.

Most days they wake up themselves
they think. Surfacing he'll stretch out
a hand, find me and slap me down
before I've emitted a sound.
He'll groan and allow himself five
more minutes. There'll be no alarm
this morning, he's in control.
When he glances my way, my face
is impassive. Of the good leader,
whose objective has been achieved,
they say: 'We did this ourselves'.

Too Long at the Fair

Delayed, at first I assumed as a boy,
by some insignificant accident,
nobody's fault – a bus coming late,
the mindless hours shopping always takes.

But then remembering where he'd gone
I couldn't believe that ribbons and stuff
would have worried him much, once he was there
enjoying himself like I did at the fair.

Next I saw him caught up in the crush
at the prizefighting, held by the dancing bear,
in too high a holiday mood to mind
who was behind him, eyeing his purse.

Pointless the warning I went to shout,
he'd already been fleeced: shrewdly barged
by a burly man whose apologies drowned
any sound the coins made changing hands.

Or perhaps it was worse: he'd simply spent
the money for presents on ale with Ned Gedge,
so what was the hurry? No rush to face her
with either the truth or a makeshift excuse.

Her version, of course, that his fingers were bound
to undo the bow and loosen her hair,
whereas being on the road to London and young,
conceivably he might have just strode on.

Or maybe, what I came to realize in time,
– unlike him – it was thugs, half a dozen
closing in, under their cloaks irresistible
reasons for going along with them.

Years, it took me, to hear through the lilt
and throb of the air her pathetic ache
for ribbons, buttons, a little straw hat.
Years more, before I was touched by that.

The Couple

Here they are, walking on the beach
on a ribbon of pebbledashed sand
the ebb-tide's exposed, turning over
arrangements, their future, the children,
a novel they've both been reading.

Years they've been coming to walk here
from autumn to spring, when swimming's
out of the question, when footpaths
are stagnant, and days on the dark side
need light, a more open horizon.

But whether they press on three-legged
or keeping a distance, some shingle,
between them, they're always a couple,
less conscious of the strength of the wind
than of feelings, their suction and flux.

Skimming down the coast their glances
focus on the far off white finger
of the Southwold light, look out
hoping for shipping, for rafts
of seabirds they still can't decipher.

Stooping now and then for the gleam
of a stone; and at some stage stopping
to take in the wavelengths, the horsepower
of swell after swell toppling over,
inklings of spray on their faces.

Lucky, they think, to be living
together here, fond of this view
of their own insignificance, skipping
back quick so they don't get their feet wet.
Hand in hand now they head for the soft

low cliff, scramble up and look round,
their goodwill confirmed, spilling over
the whole scene: the breakers, the gulls,
and the bridleway home through the trees
that eclipse Sizewell B's clean white dome.

This Time

like a priest processing, your hands
cupped in prayer, you appeared, calling
so quietly I couldn't quite hear
from the veg patch where I was bent
over beans resenting how long
picking them takes and this latest
interruption, so I was slow
to react, to catch on, and missed
seeing it close up, the shrunken
swift you were holding that somehow
had come to grief on the ground
among the goldenrod by our shed.
You'd released it before I could reach
you, tossed it up, but together
with the swift we sank, wavered and then
lifted off over the lane
between the holly and the Scots pine.

The Tightrope Wedding

We can't take our eyes off the young
couple walking to meet one another
on this cable strung between twin
towers of the castle. Fifty feet

up in the air and no net. Arms
wide, they're holding out matching
aluminium balancing poles
that are light but so long they bow slightly.

We can see how the slim, dark-haired
and suited groom bends his knees
as he leans forward shifting his weight
onto the front foot to take

his next step. The bride, we assume,
must be doing the same, somehow
holding sway over her stiff
petticoats, the satin and lace;

and, adjusting to any gust
tugging at her train, she comes on
steadily, one white shoe showing,
its soft sole curved over the rope.

They're wired up, they counterbalance
each other, but they're not one flesh yet.
We bite our lips, can't bear to look,
are glad to be distracted

by this tubby, game, down-to-earth priest
about to climb into the picture
up the fire appliance's steep
but not impossible ladder.